NORWEGIAN
a language map™

Contents

Pronunciation tip: Pronounce the phonetics just as you see them. Don't over-analyze them. Norwegian has three additional letters which are easy to pronounce:

ø *(uh)*   å *(oh)*   æ *(air)*

Speak with a Norwegian accent and, above all, enjoy yourself!

Meeting People

good day	god dag	(go)(dahg)
good morning	god morgen	(go)(mor-en)
good afternoon	god ettermiddag	(go)(et-tair-mid-ahg)
good evening	god kveld	(go)(kvel)
good night	god natt	(go)(naht)
hello/hi	hallo	(hah-loh)
please	vær så snil	(vair)(shoh)(snil)
thank you	takk	(tahk)
you're welcome	vær så god	(vair)(shoh)(go)
excuse me	unnskyld	(un-shool)
I'm sorry.	Jeg beklager.	(yay)(beh-klahg-air)
yes	ja	(yah)
no	nei	(nay)
Mr.	herr	(hair)
Mrs.	fru	(froo)
Miss	frøken	(fruhk-en)
My name is . . .	Jeg heter . . .	(yay)(het-air)
What is your name?	Hva heter du?	(vah)(het-air)(doo)
How are you?	Hvordan har du det?	(vor-dahn)(har)(doo)(deh)
well, thank you	takk, bra	(tahk)(brah)
Where are you from?	Hvor er du fra?	(vor)(ar)(doo)(frah)
I'm from	Jeg kommer fra	(yay)(kohm-air)(frah)
the U.S.A.	Amerika.	(ah-mair-ih-kuh)
Sweden.	Sverige.	(svay-ree-eh)
Denmark.	Danmark.	(dahn-mark)
Norway.	Norge.	(nor-geh)
I am . . .	Jeg er . . .	(yay)(ar)
American.	amerikaner.	(ah-mair-ih-kahn-air)
Canadian.	kanadier.	(kah-nah-dyair)
English.	englender.	(eng-len-dair)
Do you speak English?	Snakker du engelsk?	(snahk-air)(doo)(eng-elsk)
I understand.	Jeg forstår.	(yay)(for-shtor)
I do not understand.	Jeg forstår ikke.	(yay)(for-shtor)(ick-eh)
Please repeat.	Si det en gang til, takk.	(see)(deh)(en)(gahng)(til)(tahk)
good-bye	ha det bra	(hah)(deh)(brah)

Asking Questions

who	hvem	(vem)
Who is it?	Hvem er det?	(vem)(ar)(deh)
what	hva	(vah)
What is that?	Hva er det?	(vah)(ar)(deh)
how	hvordan	(vor-dahn)
how much	hvor mye	(vor)(mee-eh)
How much is it?	Hvor mye er det?	(vor)(mee-eh)(ar)(deh)
why	hvorfor	(vor-for)
when	når	(nor)
where	hvor	(vor)
Where is . . . ?	Hvor er . . . ?	(vor)(ar)

Money

Where is . . .	Hvor er . . .	(vor)(ar)
a bank?	en bank?	(en)(bahnk)
a money-exchange office?	et vekslingssted?	(et)(vek-shleengs-sted)
What is the exchange rate?	Hva er kursen?	(vah)(ar)(koors-en)
for dollars	for dollar	(for)(dohl-ar)
for traveler's checks	for reisesjekker	(for)(race-eh-shek-air)

Numbers

zero	null	(nool)
one	en/ett	(en)/(et)
two	to	(too)
three	tre	(tray)
four	fire	(fear-eh)
five	fem	(fem)
six	seks	(sex)
seven	sju	(shoe)
eight	åtte	(oh-teh)
nine	ni	(nee)
ten	ti	(tee)
11	elleve	(elv-eh)
12	tolv	(tohl)
13	tretten	(tret-ten)
14	fjorten	(fyor-ten)
15	femten	(fem-ten)
16	seksten	(sigh-ten)
17	sytten	(suh-ten)
18	atten	(ah-ten)
19	nitten	(neet-ten)
20	tjue	(hyoo-eh)
30	tretti	(tret-tee)
40	førti	(fur-tee)
50	femti	(fem-tee)
60	seksti	(sex-tee)
70	sytti	(soo-tee)
80	åtti	(oh-tee)
90	nitti	(neet-tee)
100	hundre	(huhn-dreh)
500	fem hundre	(fem)(huhn-dreh)
1,000	tusen	(too-sen)
5,000	fem tusen	(fem)(too-sen)

Mail

Where is . . .	Hvor er . . .	(vor)(ar)
the post office?	postkontoret?	(post-kohn-tor-eh)
a mailbox?	en postkasse?	(en)(post-kah-seh)
a letter	et brev	(et)(brave)
a postcard	et postkort	(et)(post-koort)
a package	en pakke	(en)(pahk-eh)
a stamp	et frimerke	(et)(free-mair-keh)
How much does a stamp cost?	Hvor mye koster et frimerke?	(vor)(mee-eh)(kohst-air)(et)(free-mair-keh)
by airmail	med flypost	(meh)(flee-post)
to America	til Amerika	(til)(ah-mair-ih-kuh)
to England	til England	(til)(eng-lahn)
I would like to buy . . .	Jeg vil gjerne kjøpe . . .	(yay)(vil)(yairn-eh)(hyuhp-eh)

Telephone

Hello	Hallo	(hah-loh)
Where is . . .	Hvor er . . .	(vor)(ar)
a telephone?	en telefon?	(en)(tay-leh-fohn)
a telephone booth?	en telefonkiosk?	(en)(tay-leh-fohn-hyohsk)
I would like to call . . .	Jeg vil gjerne ringe . . .	(yay)(vil)(yairn-eh)(ring-eh)
to Canada	til Kanada	(til)(kah-nah-dah)
to the U. S. A.	til Amerika	(til)(ah-mair-ih-kuh)
to Oslo	til Oslo	(til)(oh-shloh)
May I speak to . . .	Kan jeg snakke med . . .	(kahn)(yay)(snahk-eh)(meh)

Dining Out

(froh-kohst) **frokost** breakfast

(luhnsh) **lunsj** lunch

(mid-ahg) **middag** dinner

(tahk) (for) (mah-ten) **Takk for maten!** Thanks for the meal!

Where is . . .	Hvor er . . .	(vor)(ar)
a restaurant?	en restaurant?	(en)(res-tuh-rahng)
a pastry shop?	et konditori?	(et)(kohn-dih-tor-ee)
a café?	en kafé?	(en)(kah-fay)
a pub?	en pub?	(en)(poob)
I would like to make a reservation.	Jeg vil gjerne bestille.	(yay)(vil)(yairn-eh)(beh-stil-eh)
I have a reservation.	Jeg har bestilt.	(yay)(har)(beh-stilt)
I would like to order . . .	Jeg vil gjerne bestille . . .	(yay)(vil)(yairn-eh)(beh-stil-eh)
appetizers	forretter	(for-ret-air)
eggs	egg	(egg)
vegetables	grønnsaker	(gruhn-sahk-air)
soup	suppe	(suhp-eh)
a salad	en salat	(en)(sah-laht)
cold buffet	kaldtbord	(kahlt-boor)
open-faced sandwiches	smørbrød	(smur-bruh)
fish	fisk	(fisk)
meat	kjøtt	(hyuht)
poultry	fugl	(fool)
dessert	dessert	(des-air)
beverages	drikkevarer	(drik-eh-var-air)
a knife	en kniv	(en)(kneev)
a fork	en gaffel	(en)(gah-fel)
a spoon	en skje	(en)(shay)
a napkin	en serviett	(en)(sair-vee-et)
the waiter	kelneren	(kel-nair-en)
the waitress	frøken	(fruhk-en)
the menu	spisekartet	(spees-eh-kart-eh)
the bill	regningen	(rine-in-en)
the tip	drikkepenger	(drik-eh-peng-air)

To obtain the maximum benefit from your "*language map*™" consider purchasing a copy of **NORWEGIAN** *in 10 minutes a day*®.

Both the "*language map*™" series and the "*10 minutes a day*®" series by Kristine K. Kershul are available from your **local** bookseller or from:

Bilingual Books, Inc.
1719 West Nickerson Street, Seattle, WA 98119 USA
(800) 488-5068 or (206) 284-4211 • FAX (206) 284-3660
E-mail: info@bilingualbooks.org • http://www.bilingualbooks.org

ISBN 978-0-944502-12-9 $9.95 U.S.
9 780944 502129

Shopping

Where is . . .	Hvor er . . .	(vor)(ar)
a department store?	et magasin?	(et)(mah-gah-seen)
a laundromat?	et vaskeri?	(et)(vahsk-air-ee)
a pharmacy?	et apotek?	(et)(ah-poh-take)
a grocery store?	en matbutikk?	(en)(maht-boo-teek)
a news-stand?	en kiosk?	(en)(hyohsk)
a bakery?	et bakeri?	(et)(bah-kair-ee)
a travel agency?	et reisebyrå?	(et)(race-eh-bew-roh)
a pastry shop?	et konditori?	(et)(kohn-dih-tor-ee)
I need . . .	Jeg trenger . . .	(yay)(treng-air)
Do you have . . . ?	Har du . . . ?	(har)(doo)
How much does it cost?	Hva koster det?	(vah)(kohst-air)(deh)
too expensive	for dyr	(for)(dewr)
I'll take it.	Jeg tar det.	(yay)(tar)(deh)
Do you take	Tar du	(tar)(doo)
credit cards?	kreditkort?	(kray-deet-koort)
traveler's checks?	reisesjekker?	(race-eh-shek-air)
I would like to buy . . .	Jeg vil gjerne kjøpe . . .	(yay)(vil)(yairn-eh) (hyuhp-eh)
postcards	postkort	(post-koort)
souvenirs	suvenirer	(soo-veh-neer-air)
socks	sokker	(sohk-air)
deodorant	deodorant	(day-oh-doh-rahnt)
cheese	ost	(ohst)
wine	vin	(veen)
toothpaste	en tannkrem	(en)(tahn-krame)
aspirin	aspirin	(ahs-peer-een)
presents	gaver	(gahv-air)
shampoo	shampoo	(shahm-poo)
a liter of . . .	en liter . . .	(en)(leet-air)
a kilogram . . .	en kilo . . .	(en)(hyee-loh)

Sightseeing and Museums

Where is . . .	Hvor er . . .	(vor)(ar)
the museum?	museet?	(moo-say-eh)
the city center?	sentrum?	(sent-rum)
the cathedral?	domkirken?	(dome-hyeer-ken)
the tourist office?	turistkontoret?	(toor-ist-kohn-tor-et)
the tour bus?	bussen?	(boos-en)
the concert hall?	konserthuset?	(kohn-sairt-hoos-et)
How much does a ticket cost?	Hva koster en billett?	(vor)(kohst-air)(en)(bil-let)
art	kunst	(koonst)
music	musikk	(moo-seek)
ballet	ballett	(bahl-let)
opera	opera	(oh-pair-uh)
symphony	symfoni	(soom-fohn-ee)
concert	konsert	(kohn-sairt)
modern	moderne	(moh-dair-neh)
old	gammel	(gahm-el)
good	god	(go)
bad	dårlig	(dor-lee)
open	åpen	(oh-pent)
closed	lukket	(luhk-et)
left	venstre	(ven-streh)
right	høyre	(huh-oy-reh)

Transportation

a map/the map	et kart/karten	(et)(kart)/(kart-en)
a car/the car	en bil/bilen	(en)(beel)/(beel-en)
a bicycle/the bicycle	en sykkel/sykkelen	(en)(seek-el)/(seek-el-en)
a motorcycle/ the motorcycle	en motorsykkel/ motorsykkelen	(en)(moh-tor-seek-el) (moh-tor-seek-el-en)
a train/the train	et tog/toget	(en)(tohg)/(tohg-eh)
a train station	en jernbanestasjon	(en)(yairn-bahn-eh-stah-shohn)
the airplane	flyet	(flee-et)
the airport	flyplassen	(flee-plahs-en)
Where is . . .	Hvor er . . .	(vor)(ar)
the bus stop?	bussholdeplassen?	(boos-hold-eh-plahs-en)
the subway stop?	trikkeholdeplassen?	(trik-eh-hold-eh-plahs-en)
a ticket/the ticket	en billett/billetten	(en)(bil-let)/(bil-let-en)
one-way	enkelt	(eng-kelt)
round trip	tur-retur	(toor-ray-toor)
arrival	ankomst	(ahn-kohmst)
departure	avgang	(ahv-gahng)
the gas station	en bensinstasjon	(en)(ben-seen-stah-shohn)
I would like a ticket to . . .	Jeg vil gjerne en billett til . . .	(yay)(vil)(yairn-eh)(en) (bil-let)(til)
How much is a ticket to . . . ?	Hva koster en billett til . . .	(vah)(kohst-air)(en) (bil-let)(til)
Where do I get off?	Hvor stiger jeg av?	(vor)(steeg-air)(yay)(ahv)
Stop here, please!	Kan du stoppe her?	(kahn)(doo)(stohp-eh)(hair)

(en) (boos)/ (boos-en)		(en) (trik) (trik-en)
en buss / bussen		en trikk / trikken
a bus the bus		a streetcar the streetcar

(en) (droh-sheh)/ (droh-shen)	
en drosje /	drosjen
a taxi	the taxi

(tay-bahn-en)	(go) (toor)
T-banen	God tur!
the subway	Have a good trip!

Hotels and Room Service

Where is . . .	Hvor er . . .	(vor)(ar)
a hotel?	et hotell?	(et)(hoh-tel)
a hut/chalet?	en hytte?	(en)(hew-teh)
a hostel?	et herberge?	(et)(hair-bairg-eh)
a house?	et hus?	(et)(hoos)
vacancy	ledig rom	(lay-dee)(rohm)
no vacancy	ingen ledighet	(ing-en)(lay-dee-het)
expensive	dyr	(dewr)
inexpensive	billig	(bil-ee)
the key	nøkkelen	(nuhk-el-en)
a bed	ei seng	(ay)(seng)
a pillow	ei pute	(ay)(poo-teh)
a comforter	ei dyne	(ay)(dee-neh)
a towel	et håndkle	(et)(hohn-klay)
I would like	Jeg vil gjerne ha	(yay)(vil)(yairn-eh)(hah)
a single room	et enkeltrom	(et)(eng-kelt-rohm)
a double room	et dobbeltrom	(et)(dobb-elt-rohm)
a quiet room	et rolig rom	(et)(roh-lee)(rohm)
with a bath	med bad	(meh)(bahd)
with a shower	med dusj	(meh)(dush)
for one night	for en natt	(for)(en)(naht)
for two nights	for to netter	(for)(too)(net-air)
for tonight	for i natt	(for)(ee)(naht)
I have a reservation.	Jeg har bestilt.	(yay)(har)(beh-stilt)
I do not have a reservation.	Jeg har ikke bestilt.	(yay)(har)(ick-eh) (beh-stilt)
How much does the room cost?	Hvor mye koster rommet?	(vor)(mee-eh) (kohst-air)(rohm-et)
Is breakfast included?	Er frokost inkludert?	(ar)(froh-kohst) (in-kloo-dairt)
I'm in room number . . .	Jeg er i rom . . .	(yay)(ar)(ee)(rohm)
Sleep well!	Sov godt!	(sohv)(goht)

	(yay) (ar) (suhl-ten)
	Jeg er sulten.
	I'm hungry.

	(yay) (ar) (tursht)
	Jeg er tørst.
	I'm thirsty.

Time

What time is it?	Hvor mye er klokka?	(vor)(mee-eh)(ar)(klohk-uh)
It is	Den er	(den)(ar)
four o'clock	fire	(fear-eh)
five o'clock	fem	(fem)
early	tidlig	(tee-lee)
late	sent	(sent)
minute	minutt	(min-oot)
hour	time	(teem-eh)
day	dag	(dahg)
week	uke	(ook-eh)
month	måned	(moh-ned)
year	år	(or)

Calendar

When?	Når?	(nor)
on Monday	mandag	(mahn-dahg)
on Tuesday	tirsdag	(teersh-dahg)
on Wednesday	onsdag	(ohns-dahg)
on Thursday	torsdag	(torsh-dahg)
on Friday	fredag	(fray-dahg)
on Saturday	lørdag	(lur-dahg)
on Sunday	søndag	(suhn-dahg)
today	i dag	(ee)(dahg)
yesterday	i går	(ee)(gor)
tomorrow	i morgen	(ee)(mor-en)
morning	morgen	(mor-en)
afternoon	ettermiddag	(et-tair-mid-ahg)
evening	kveld	(kvel)
night	natt	(naht)
in January	januar	(yah-noo-ar)
in February	februar	(fay-broo-ar)
in March	mars	(marsh)
in April	april	(ah-preel)
in May	mai	(my)
in June	juni	(yoo-nee)
in July	juli	(yoo-lee)
in August	august	(ow-goost)
in September	september	(sep-tem-bair)
in October	oktober	(ohk-toh-bair)
in November	november	(noh-vem-bair)
in December	desember	(des-em-bair)

Life's Little Emergencies

Where is the lavatory?	Hvor er toaletten?	(vor)(ar)(toh-ah-let-en)
entrance forbidden	adgang forbudt	(ahd-gahng)(for)(buht)
I'm lost.	Jeg har gått meg vill.	(yay)(har)(goht)(my)(vil)
I have lost . . .	Jeg har mistet . . .	(yay)(har)(mist-et)
my passport	mit pass	(mit)(pahs)
my ticket	min billet	(meen)(bil-let)
my wallet	mi lommebok	(mee)(lohm-eh-bohk)
my handbag	mi håndveske	(mee)(hohnd-vesk-eh)
Please call . . .	Kan du ringe . . .	(kahn)(doo)(ring-eh)
a doctor	en lege	(en)(lay-geh)
an ambulance	en ambulanse	(en)(ahm-boo-lahns-eh)
I'm ill.	Jeg er dårlig.	(yay)(ar)(dor-lee)
I have a pain here.	Jeg har vondt her.	(yay)(har)(vohnt)(hair)

(poh-lih-tee)
politi
police

(en) (lay-geh)
en lege
a doctor

(seek-eh-hoos-et)
sykehuset
the hospital

(for-shvin)
Forsvinn!
Go away!

(yelp)
Hjelp!
help